# Making Money Online
*A Beginners Guide to Marketing, Ecommerce, Drop Shipping and Investing*

# Introduction

I want to thank you and congratulate you for downloading the book, *"Making Money Online"*.

This book has lots of actionable information on how to make money online using different strategies.

It is now a proven fact: you can make real money online. Even as many people continue to view the internet as a sheer waste of time in terms of earning a living, the internet has repeatedly proven itself a profitable area for anyone from any part of the globe to earn a decent income. There is a reason why the internet is undoubtedly the one industry that is making the most number of millionaires in the modern times (a staggering estimated 90%)!

Even if you don't make it to 'millionairehood', the truth is that you can make lots of money very fast (if you put the necessary effort of course) thanks the internet's ability to overcome some of the challenges of brick and mortar business models.

The thing is; there is a lot of info out there hyping the idea of being an internet millionaire in a few months or years. But the truth is that without specifics on how to actually go about it, even making your first $50 can seem like an impossible feat leave alone a million dollars.

So how do you do about it? Well, that's where this book comes in. It will help you to discover the steps you can take to realize your dream of making money online.

Thanks again for downloading this book. I hope you enjoy it!

# Table of Contents

Before we can discuss the specifics of how to actually make money online, it is important to start by understanding what making money online really means just to make sure we are on the same page.

# Making Money Online: A Brief Overview

*What Does Making Money Online Entail?*

For many people, the idea of making money online could be biased based on when they first learnt that they can make money online. For instance, if you discovered that you can make money online by working on different projects for clients (whether in an online marketplace or not), you are likely to believe that for you to make money online, you ought to actually 'work' online. But the truth is, you don't have to 'work' online to make money online. You could develop a system that enables you to earn money online by selling such things like digital products, which essentially means you don't get to exchange your hours for money (work). For others, working online may mean dedicating 8 or so hours actually 'working' online. And for others, the idea of making money online brings images of them at the beach with loved ones while money is flowing into their bank accounts!

From the explanation, it is clear that making money online can take different forms i.e. a form where you exchange your hours for money (in simple terms, you are actually working) and a form where you set up systems upfront then make money on an ongoing basis without exchanging your hours for money.

Whichever approach you use to make your money online, you can bet that you will derive a number of benefits some of which include:

- *Location Independence*

The fact that the internet is everywhere makes it very easy to make money from anywhere in the world i.e. at home, while traveling, from a coffee shop, etc. All you need is an internet connection and a device to connect to the internet to do whatever needs to be done to make money. With that, you can save the time and money you otherwise might have had to use commuting to work.

- *Cost And Bureaucracies*

Unlike in the typical (offline) world where you might have to spend several thousand dollars before you make your first sale, you don't need much to start making a steady income online. For some models (e.g. where you exchange your hours for money), you don't even need to spend any money to start. And for others, you need very little amount to start e.g. $20 for hosting and domain.

- *Not Too Time Consuming*

You can make money online on a part time basis. Given that you don't have a fixed work schedule (e.g. the typical 9-5), this means you can still go on with your day job while making money online on the side. And the good thing about making money online is that depending on the model you choose, you may end up making more money online (while working part time) than you make in your 9-5 job!

- *Potential*

The potential on how much money you can make online is mind-boggling. Some individuals are making as much as hundreds of thousands a month without any staff for instance (working part time), a feat that is hard to pull while working offline. The fact that you can leverage on technology to automate many aspects makes the earning potential limitless.

So how exactly do you start to make money online?

From the explanation above, it is clear that there are active streams of online income i.e. where you exchange your hours for money (just like in a typical offline 9-5 job) and there are streams where how much you make is not tied to / proportional to your time input. Since active income streams are the easiest to start (especially if you have a skill that others may want) because it requires zero cash to start, we will start by discussing how to make money using active income streams.

# How to Make Money Online:

# Possible Active Income Streams

Like as stated, there are many ways to make money online. They all fall into two main categories: *passive* and *active income streams*.

Let us begin with active income streams.

By definition, an active income is income you get after offering services. This type of income may be in the form of wages, tips, and commissions. In this case, an active income is an income from businesses you participate in materially, and the income stops streaming in when you stop working.

We will talk about ways through which you will be making money online this way. At the beginning, which is where we are, I will not expect you to have a website or a product to sell. I will therefore introduce something that that does require that:

## Take Surveys

Countless sites on the internet offer users the ability to generate income for taking online surveys. I suggest you start with toluna.com if you want to grab these opportunities. If you like this model of making money, you can also try Cash Crate, which is also a good option. Apart from receiving pay for taking surveys, these platforms also offer cashbacks and other quick online income rewards.

Most companies and businesses need surveys. They outsource these surveys to professional survey companies. These companies then gather a database of people and then interact with suitable respondents for every survey while offering money as an incentive.

For this money making model, you need to get the right, legit sites because many scammers out have sweet deals. I-Say is one of the best paying survey companies. It pays people in points. Most surveys have a point worth of 5 and 250 points and as a member, you get an average of four surveys per month. For a £10 voucher, you typically require 1380 points.

## Flipping Domains

Flipping domains is the art of buying and selling domain names. A domain is a subset of the internet controlled by a company or a person by sharing a common suffix. Some domain names out there are worth a lot of money. Business.com and Hotel.com are good examples that have sold for $7 million and $11 million respectively.

Of course, coming across such great domain names might seem like a long shot, but you can still generate a decent income by choosing to flip domains as a part-time online business.

In this regard, I suggest you:

*Step 1: Find Hot Keywords and Target Local Domain Names*
Start by focusing on getting hot keywords domains that would interest buyers. I suggest you go for a domain name containing acceptable traffic – perhaps having about 10,000 searches per month. Tools such as the Niche Finder Software can help you out with this.

Appreciate that local search engine optimization has grown and for this reason, targeting local names is uniquely profitable. Everyone wants to see their business thrive on the first page of Google Search results. Getting the right keyword optimized domain helps local businesses do this.

*Step 2: Look For an Existing Domain Name*

It can also be quite profitable to buy existing domain names. Finding such domains is relatively easy; just ensure you select names that have good traffic and avoid names with special numbers or characters because like most domain-flipping experts, I believe they are not likely sell.

After getting the right domain name, go to the next step:

*Step 3: Contact the Owners*

First, you have to confirm that you can communicate with and locate the domain owner. There are several ways to get the domain owner's contact details:

*1. Scan the site for contacts. You might find a 'the site may be for sale' link somewhere on the website.*

*2. The internet archive*

*3. If you do not find it on the site, use the directory: 'who is' (I like domaintools.com for this)*

After getting the contact details, negotiate the prices. This process requires good negotiating skills: here are some cool tips to help you do this safely and effectively.

*Step 4: Wait*

Do not sell the site immediately. Flipping domains is never about making quick money. Take all the time you need and in the meantime, look at your parked domain as investment. During this period, a good thing to do would be to try developing it. Check out the tips on this good site that will help you add value to your newly acquired domain.

*Step 5: Sell it*

When you think your domain has increased in value, look for a good place to sell it. One of the best places to sell it would be Sedo. Sedo is recognized as one of the largest market places for domain sales and most domain name buyers worldwide always consider it first when they want to make such a purchase.

Other places you can sell your domain name include the following:

Flippa

Cax.com

Afternic

Brand Bucket

eBay

4.cn

Hunting Moon

Aftermarket.com

Your own website

# Website Design & Development

Many businesses and individuals are always in need of websites to provide clients important information about their services and products. If you are good at designing websites, you can offer your services by either building one from scratch or upgrading one already in existence somewhere on the internet. Quite often, business owners will rely on your knowhow for guidance on selecting the best template for their site – something that lets you be creative on the job.

If you do not how to design websites, this place can help you learn how to do it. Furthermore, there are many design jobs on the internet. As you try to discover them, you can start by checking out:

- Upwork.com

- Fiverr.com

- 99designs.com

- Freelancer.com

- Peopleperhour.com

- Designcrowd.com

- Guru.com

- WarriorForum.Com

- BlackHatWorld.Com

---

## Graphic Design

Just like web design, in this regard, you can offer numerous services like illustrations, logo design, banner adverts, posters, info graphics, and flyers, among many others. As a freelance graphic designer though, you have to be creative and always strive to sharpen your skills so you can offer quality design services that attract regular clients.

In addition to the sites indicated above, you can check the following sites for graphic design jobs:

Coroflot
Authentic Jobs
Creative Hotlist
Smashing Jobs
Design Observer
Dribbble
Krop
Simply Hired
AIGA Design Jobs
Behance

## Proofreading And Editing

Many educationalists and students are always on the lookout for people who can help them correct spelling and grammatical errors in their academic projects, business articles, blog posts and SEO articles. If you are good at making documents more comprehensive by identifying errors and making relevant changes to them, this is your job. Additionally, you can extend your editing knowledge to books and online magazines too. Here is a list of companies that will offer you proofreading and editing jobs.

## Freelance Writing/Ghostwriting

The web is driven by content (especially text because users use text to search for content on search engines). If you have a knack for writing, you can make money by offering your writing services to customers around the world. You can write articles, blog posts, ebooks and other types of content. Some of the places where you can get writing work include:

**Marketplaces Like**
Upwork.com
Fiverr.com
Freelancer.com
Peopleperhour.com
Guru.com
**Content Farms**
iWriter.com
Textbroker.com
eCopywriters.com
Demandstudios.com
Wordsofworth.com
WriterAccess.com

Scripted.com
Writtent.com
And many others
**Forums Like**
WarriorForum.Com
BlackHatWorld.Com

You can check out other sites here.

## Translation

As the world increasingly becomes a global village, the
demand for translation services is constantly on the rise. This
presents a unique opportunity for those who understand
several languages. You can offer your services on:
**Marketplaces like**
Upwork.com
Mytranslation.com
Proz.com
Translatorscafe.Com
Translatorpub.Com
Fiverr.com
Freelancer.com
Peopleperhour.com
Guru.com

## Transcription

Another service you can offer for pay online is transcription
i.e. where you listen to a recorded audio then write down
what the speaker is saying. You can check out some of the
largest market places like:
Upwork.com

Fiverr.com
Freelancer.com
Peopleperhour.com
Guru.com
You can check out this link for more.

These are not the only ways through which you can make
money online by actually working on individual projects
where you exchange your hours for money. The list is endless
including running errands for people (virtual assisting), data
entry, moderation, etc. You can learn more here.

Besides working online (exchanging your hours for money),
you can also make money online passively. The next part of
the book will discuss some ways to make passive income
online.

# How to Make Money Online:

# Possible Passive Income Streams

In this part of the book, we shall talk about the other category of income: *passive income streams*

By definition, a passive income broadly refers to the revenue you generate when you are not actively working. The other name for a passive income is a *residual income.*

A passive income pays you regardless of whether or not you do any meaningful work. To get the ball rolling, however, you may do quite a lot of work upfront but eventually, you will get to a point where money flows into your account even when you are not actively working.

Here are various passive income ideas you can implement online:

## Revenue Sharing

If writing is your hobby, that is all you require here. You can earn good money from writing high quality articles and submitting them to various places on sites that share revenues with their authors. This viable option is one you can use to get started immediately. The following are the top ways to earn money from online revenue sharing:

## Hub Pages

HubPages.com is a community that refers to its writers as 'hubbers.' Once you sign up, HubPages will assign you a subdomain where you can post content rich articles usually known as 'Hubs'.

As a hubber, your main source of revenue is Google AdSense. You will therefore need an AdSense account and other vehicles of advertising such as eBay, Kontera, and Amazon Affiliate programs.

On HubPages, there is a 60:40 split of revenue and there exists four ways through which you can earn money. These include the HubPages Earnings program (HP), Amazon, eBay, and the HubPages referral program. HP helps you earn money from ads displayed by AdSense and HubPages.

By promoting eBay and Amazon products, you can earn a commission for each product sold. The affiliate program helps you earn money by referring people to hubs. This allows you to earn 15% of the total revenue Hub generates.

## Infobarrel

I have developed a liking for Infobarrel because its earnings program allows publishers to keep most of the money their articles generate. As a publisher, you keep 75% of the total revenue generated from the ads displayed on your articles. Some time back, payment for these ads would from AdSense and other advertisers but since a Google AdSense account is not something everyone can get, InfoBarrel decided to change that. It now pays writers directly. You will only require a PayPal account.

Moreover, InfoBarrel forums usually have the 'InfoBarrel Earnings Reports,' a regular thread that may interest you if you are wondering how much cash other writers on this platform actually make.

## Quick Income Perks

In this category, we will be discussing some methods that have one thing in common: *you earn good money from completing simple online tasks.*
I have decided to include these in the book so that we can dispel, once and for all, any doubt about the internet and its ease to earn an active income from it. Once you make your first dollar online, how you view the entire thing will suddenly change. Check out the following online income generating ways:

### Cashbacks

The idea behind generating income through cashback sites is very straightforward: you receive a reward for buying or using products you plan to purchase anyway. These sites will pay you for clicking through them, going to retailers, and spending.
For instance, when you check out eBates.com, you will find over 2,000 stores you can shop from – including Calvin Klein, Walmart, and Sears.
Once you register with all the cashback sites you desire, search for deals on offer by checking your favorite financial services firms or preferred retailers. Next, click the provided link.

After seeing a deal you like, visit the retailer by clicking on the link on the cashback site. Next, complete the purchase and right there, the retailer will send you a commission to your cashback account. The cashback site will later transfer part of this cash into your PayPal account.

## Affiliate Marketing

Affiliate marketing applies a simple idea: you generate online income by promoting other people's or company's products and earn a commission on each sales you make. Theoretically, all you have to do is partner up with affiliate programs, acquire their affiliate links, and begin promoting them on whichever platform you wish.

That sounds very simple. Well, the idea is simple, but you will have to do more than just post affiliate links on Twitter, Facebook, your website, and so on. While using this strategy may reward you with a sale or two, your best bet at a steady and tangible stream of income is to look at it differently:

If you are looking for a consistent income, you will have to think about building a good and lasting relationship with your audience, something requiring a strategic approach.

Try to find ways to do that. One way you could achieve this is by building a personal email list from your blog. When you do that, say by using a service like AWeber.com or Mail Chimp, you will be creating a list of people you think trust you and your ability to recommend great affiliate products.

Now that you know that, let us discuss the top ways of earning money in this category

## ClickBank Products

Touted as the largest online marketplace for digital products, ClickBank.com is a platform that uses a great measure to represent how well a particular product sells – something referred to as 'gravity'. The gravity of a product is based on the number of sales made and how recent they were.
You however need to know that:
**1.** Until an account shows a minimum of five sales, ClickBank withholds payments of any balances.
**2.** If you sell but fail to generate earnings for an extended period, you become liable to a penalty.
Even though this means your affiliate earnings could drop to zero, ClickBank is still worth a try because it becomes easier to work with when you get the hang of it and many people are making good money off it.

## Amazon Products

You can also sign up for Amazon Affiliate Program and promote Amazon's online store, which besides being well known, is quite dependable. One of the biggest advantages to working with Amazon is that everybody out there knows it. The commission you will get for promoting its products starts from 4% even though some products can go up to 8% depending on the number of sales you make.
Essentially, when you send someone to Amazon (when they click your link), you receive a commission on any product they buy within 24hours even if that person opted to buy a different product as well (which means extra commissions for you). For instance, if you promote an Amazon's laptop and the person you directed to Amazon decides to buy a phone too, you will receive commissions for both products.

## Commission Junction Products

Commission Junction or 'CJ' as many know it is one of the largest and oldest affiliate networks in existence. Here, you will find most well established merchants, something that is a big advantage especially if you are looking to promote bigger brands. CJ comes with another advantage: apart from the usual pay-per-sale offer, you will find other offers such as pay-per-lead.
Pay per-lead refers to the payments offered for the leads generated at the destination site. If the visitors you direct happens to sign up (usually when it involves contact info and maybe some demographic info), you get this bonus payment. Other affiliate marketplaces include:
JvZoo.com
ShareASale.com
EJunkie.com
LinkShare.com
FlexOffers.com

## Start a Unique/Creative Online Business

Have you ever wanted to own a business? Well, the internet has made owning a business dummy easy. You could begin a side business as you continue doing your part-time or full time job. For instance, if you are a web or graphic designer, you could work on starting your web or graphic design business on the side. Do you love making unique fabric designs? You could begin selling your designs online.

Starting an online business is one of the most difficult things anyone can try but if you believe in yourself, what you earn from it could eventually see you quitting your part-time or full-time job.

One good example of an online business is creating a listicle blog. Such a simple idea that can take up less than an hour of your time each week and probably $20 in costs can over time earn you some good money. You could create captivating content by looking for inspirational, funny, and any other type of stories on Imgur, Reddit, and Facebook to rewrite, and perhaps add some more detail before publishing it on your site.

Many sites have done this and achieved immense success. One example is Viralnova.com that sold for $100 million (it was making more than $400k in ad revenue per month). When you use sites such as StumbleUpon, Twitter, and Facebook for promotion, you can eventually generate organic traffic that in a few months can get you up to a minimum of 50K unique visits each month. Once you get to this point, you can use AdSense to monetize the traffic and generate revenue

## EBook Publishing

Many content creators, amateur writers, and even bloggers have done it and they love it! You do not need the brain of a rocket scientist to create a 50 page (or less) eBook. However, generating sales from your eBook every month for say between $500 to $1,000 through online networking, your own SEO optimized blog, or even guest posting is a possible.

**TIP:** You have to be careful about pricing: be on the lookout for niches where the audience targeted is likely not likely to pay $5 for an eBook.

You can also repackage your eBook for sale on Amazon and iBook where you will find many interested buyers.

# E-Commerce and Drop Shipping Products

If you are hell-bent on making a real passive income online, this is probably the greatest idea you could get but remember, compared to many other ideas, this one requires a lot of upfront work.

Dropshipping is a method in supply chain management where you, the retailer, does not keep the goods but transfers the client orders (and the details of shipment) to another retailer, wholesaler, or even a manufacturer who then processes the order and ships the item to the end user/customer.

To engage in dropshipping, simply find a product people generally find hard to buy (from specialized bedding to latest robots or magic trick supplies, anything goes) online, and then start your own online store.

Next, work out a direct dropshipping arrangement with a trusted provider and there you have it! (There is a lot to learn about how this works so please check here to read everything you need to know about drop shipping – including how to source for suppliers and pick niche products and markets). Nonetheless, you have to look for products within the price range of $50 - $200 because such products are cheaper to ship and remain stable (do not run out of demand or require frequent updating) over time and cannot be price-shopped online.

For instance, aqua blue bedding that contains a different mix of thread count, type of material, and so on is very difficult to overprice whereas a branded camera is easy to do so.

# 11: YouTube Ads

If you are not into blogging because perhaps you think that compared to YouTube, it is not as easy to generate views, you are right.

Actually, in the average attention span, people prefer watching ten videos to reading two blog posts, and as you may have noticed, Google search results rarely fail to display YouTube videos in any search results (which probably means it favors YouTube).

This is a good passive income opportunity particularly when you consider the time it will take to create a simple video: on average, creating a YouTube video on any given topic takes 5 minutes.

Once you create a video on say a technical topic and post it, the vast online space will not lack someone somewhere looking for a solution to the same problem you tackled. Once the person starts watching the video, when relevant and applicable ad pops up for a product that is perfect for that particular problem, the viewer is bound to click through. The more expensive the product is, the more ad revenue you generate.

To make this work, however, create YouTube account, channel, and regularly start posting as many videos as possible. The next thing is to monetize.

Set up your Google AdSense account if you do not already have one, and then link it to your YouTube account. You will receive money from YouTube per advertisement click and per view. The more views your video generates, the more potential of ads click and views, and the higher your income shall be.

# A Book Reviews Website

We will use Amazon affiliate links for the monetization strategy here. Amazon pays well- for a book selling in the range of $10-$30 – 5-10% is not bad – because a dollar here and there can add up.

Let us compare this with writing content with AdSense revenue in mind. With enough hard work, hundreds of reviews, and thousands of visitors per week, you can earn upwards of $500 each month.

Fundamentally, a reviews site requires high ranking in Google and possibly building a list of emails to send your reviews to. You therefore need to achieve these two, which you can do by first choosing a very specific niche.

I am thinking early stage entrepreneurs. Take startup daily as an example: Startup Daily is a website that reviews a new businesses book each day and places corresponding Amazon links in the review.

If you want to generate a few dollars every month, affiliating books is a good idea. You can learn more information about Amazon affiliates so you know more about which products to affiliate, as well as how to do it in a way that seems many people clicking on your links.

# License Your Ideas

If you do not feel confident about risking your capital to create and sell a product, but you have product ideas that fill real market gaps, you could become an inventor.

For this money making model, you have to consider the following though:

*1. License fees for unproven or generally unknown inventors can only be a couple percentages at most*

*2. Many ideas are generally not worth anything, and those you can license have to be very specific if they are going to add value.*
*3. This will require knowledge in networking and pitching*

If you are a technically minded person who is always noticing flaws in existing products, and can punch up a few diagrams and literature (on an idea) that is very specific so that it adds value and worth, and then even patent it, that could be all you need to enter into a lifestyle driven by license fees.

All the steps you need to licensing your ideas are on this site.

## Software and Web Apps

From online productivity tools, to WordPress themes, to something more industry specific such as online billing service for engineers, this is a niche you can exploit and make some serious coin. The good thing is that there are professionals out there waiting to do all the heavy lifting for you while you market and sell the software online.

**NOTE:** If you do not have any skills or background in all this, going for software products can be risky if you are aiming to create a passive income stream.

However, going with software is not entirely difficult. For instance, coming up with a package of PowerPoint graphics for others to use for quick prototyping of apps, creating a simple WordPress theme (niched up), or hiring a contractor on Upwork to do it for you for $1,400 – that also counts – makes it very easy.

When you have created your software or web app, and you are ready to sell it, I recommend you first go through the following tips of selling software so that you get the most of it.

The best part of all this is that there exists very many places where you can sell software. If you need to find the top ten, click here.

## Online Courses and Membership Sites

Before anything, I think you need to know that we are talking about a multimedia-driven, members-only website. This requires a lot of work. It requires many words, many hours of video and audio, and probably more than 15 resources to go with it. In other words, nobody would dare call you lazy for looking for an expert to do the heavy lifting or finding someone to help you out with it.

However, the results are astounding. By charging $200, you will enjoy a bank rate of about 1% (you would be surprised to know how many people love videos and practical resources) and a quarter of the entire content created is used for search engine optimization, meaning that as the product was being created, the market side of things was also being done. Therefore, if you have a niche you are very knowledgeable about, you could just build a comprehensive course on it and hire experts to help you out along the way in areas you are not very conversant with or don't have time to work on. You could also structure the course/membership site in a way that allows you to charge about $20-$50 for things such as new resources, updates, mentoring, and perhaps member's only forums.

# Conclusion

Thank you again for downloading this book!

As stated earlier, there are hundreds of ways to make money online. This book has merely covered what I consider the best ways to make money online today. In summary, we have looked at:

## Active Income Streams

Flipping domains

Website design

Graphic design

Writing

Transcription

Translating

Proofreading and editing

## Passive Income Streams

Affiliate marketing

Starting a creative online business

E-book, e-commerce and drop shipping products

YouTube ads

Book reviews website

Licensing your ideas

Software and web apps

Selling online courses and membership sites

Even if you do not implement all the ways to make money we have discussed, implementing as little as two of these ways will see you earning tons of money.

Finally, if you enjoyed this book, would you be kind enough to leave a review for this book on Amazon?

Click here to leave a review for this book on Amazon!

Thank you and good luck!

www.ingramcontent.com/pod-product-compliance
Lightning Source LLC
Chambersburg PA
CBHW070732180526
45167CB00004B/1720

* 9 7 8 1 5 4 2 8 6 7 0 5 4 *